A Pastor's
SURVIVOR
GUIDE

   FOR COLLEGE

OR

FOR CAREER

BY JAY R. ASHBAUCHER

Reid Ashbaucher Publications | Cleveland, Tennessee, USA

Reid Ashbaucher Publications
Cleveland, Tennessee U.S.A.
https://ra-publications.us

A Pastor's Survivor Guide for College or for Career

Copyright © 2022 by Jay R. Ashbaucher
All rights reserved.

No part of this publication may be reproduced, stored in a retrieval system, or transmitted in any form or by any means electronic, mechanical, photocopying, recording, or otherwise, without the prior written permission of the author.

All Scripture quotations taken from the New American Standard Bible® (NASB), Copyright © 1960, 1962, 1963, 1968, 1971, 1972, 1973, 1975, 1977, 1995 by the Lockman Foundation, unless otherwise noted. Used by permission. www.Lockman.org

Copyright © permissions can be obtained from the author through the following website: https://jay-ashbaucher.com

Cover photo "traffic-sign" by Gerd Altmann from Pixabay.com
Cover photo "graduate" by Randy Stanz from Pixabay.com
Cover photo "stone" by Elias from Pixabay.com

Interior Vector Graphics and Illustration Images by Pixabay.com

Library of Congress Control Number: 2022917404
ISBN: 978-1-7350948-6-1

Printed in the United States of America
U.S. Printing History

First Edition: September 2022

CONTENTS

Preface - p. 4
Introduction - - - - - - - - - - - - - - - - - - - p. 5
Why a Survivor Guide? (3 Reasons) p. 6
    Our corrupt natures - - - - - - - - p. 7
    Our enemy the devil - - - - - - - - p. 10
    Our contact with God - - - - - - p. 12
Does God Exist? - - - - - - - - - - - - - - - p. 14
How to Survive (4 ways) - - - - - - - - - p. 15
    Be a Christ Follower - - - - - - - - p. 16
    Understand the Bible - - - - - - p. 17
    Participate in a Group - - - - - - p. 21
    Know What and Why - - - - - - p. 25
Truth and Tolerance - - - - - - - - - - - - p. 27
Morality, Sex - - - - - - - - - - - - - - - - - - p. 33
Dating, Marriage - - - - - - - - - - - - - - - p. 37
Vocation - p. 39
How to Know God's Will - - - - - - - - - p. 41
Humanity—Who are We? - - - - - - - - p. 42
Friends and Church - - - - - - - - - - - - p. 44
Parting Comments - - - - - - - - - - - - - p. 48
You are a Winner - - - - - - - - - - - - - - p. 48
Hang in There - - - - - - - - - - - - - - - - p. 49
About the Author - - - - - - - - - - - - - - p. 51
Other Books by the Author - - - - - - - p. 52

PREFACE

This survival guide is for Christian high school graduates who may or may not have a church background and are planning to attend college or pursue some kind of vocational work and training.

The booklet may also be helpful to any graduate who is interested in spiritual things or wants to include God as a part of his or her future life journey.

In today's world, the Christian Faith and the church have not appealed to most people's interests and needs, and yet, lots of young people want to know what can best help them get through life's hard times and enable them to experience successful daily living.

Even though the church has received much criticism, Jesus is still a person many people accept as one who is wise, loving, and caring. He is one with whom anyone can have a meaningful relationship, and he is an excellent personal guide.

Because the church is Jesus' creation to do his work on earth, and there exist many good churches with people who sincerely are following Jesus, this survivor guide includes the church as an important part of the life of anyone who chooses to follow Jesus. Without reservation, I recommend knowing Jesus and his teachings as the best way to live one's life.

— Pastor Jay

INTRODUCTION

As you step up to new challenges, new freedoms, and new places, it can be a bit scary as well as exciting. This booklet explains how you can be blessed by the kind of life God wants you to have.

Life is fun, and most of us enjoy our daily experiences. But as you have, or will discover, life has its dark side, as well as its good side, and we must be prepared to know how to deal with both sides. Why should we let our aspirations for a great life fade away in the fog of an unmanaged life?

The Bible tells us about both sides of life:

> "The thief comes only to steal, and kill, and destroy; I came that they might have life, and might have it abundantly."
>
> — Jesus (John 10:10)

Although God created life to be good and beautiful, fun-filled and meaningful, we unfortunately live in a dangerous world. It is not at all uncommon for people to experience shattered and heartbroken lives, to see their potential for goodness slip away, never seeing their dreams become real.

Thus, here is a survivor guide to help you get the most out of life and to help you achieve your greatest God-given potential.

As you read, you will come across some questions that provide opportunity for you to do your own thinking and decision making.

The quotes from the Bible are to remind you of things God has to say about the subjects being discussed.

WHY A SURVIVOR GUIDE?

THREE REASONS

1. We have corrupted, self-centered natures against us.

2. We have a real live supernatural devil against us.

3. We need to maintain contact with the all-powerful and loving God who can help us.

Let's consider each one of these reasons.

REASON ONE: We have corrupted, self-centered natures against us.

All human beings have corrupt natures. Because of this, we are prone to wander from the God who created us and who can restore us. When we follow our corrupt nature, we fall prey to temptations and evils that destroy our peace and happiness, but, most of all, we are on the wrong side of God and we lose the life God meant for us to have.

Paul, a servant chosen by God, describes our corrupt nature like this:

> *"For I know that nothing good dwells in me, that is, in my flesh; for the wishing is present in me, but the doing of the good is not. I find then the principle that evil is present in me, the one who wishes to do good."* —Paul (Romans 7:18, 2l)

The Bible tells of many dangers we can fall into because of our corrupt natures. Here are some:

> *"But realize this, that <u>in the last days difficult times will come.</u> For people will be lovers of self, lovers of money, boastful, arrogant, revilers, disobedient to parents, ungrateful, unholy, unloving, irreconcilable, malicious gossips, without self-control, brutal, haters of good, treacherous, reckless, conceited, lovers of pleasure rather than lovers of God..."*
>
> — *Paul to Timothy (2 Timothy 3:1-4)*

"Now the deeds of the flesh are evident, which are: immorality, impurity, sensuality, idolatry, sorcery, enmities, strife, jealousy, outbursts of anger, disputes, dissensions, factions, envying, drunkenness, carousing, and things like these, of which I forewarn you just as I have forewarned you that those who practice such things shall not inherit the kingdom of God." (Galatians 5:19-21)

"For what is a person profited if he gains the whole world, and loses or forfeits his own soul?" — Jesus (Luke 9:25)

Most people don't generally see themselves as God does.

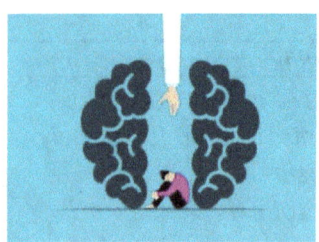

You may find some people saying things like:

"Humans are basically good."

"The moral evil in our lives is caused by our incomplete evolution into better beings."

"Human corruption is a result of social depravity, or poor environmental conditions, or faulty genetics or lack of proper education."

"If we keep working on improving ourselves with politics, education, science, and technology, we will get better."

An answer to this is:

We are more technologically advanced and educated than ever before in human history, yet evil and corruption abounds. People don't like what evil does to them, so why do they let it keep hanging around, messing up and destroying their lives? Is it because the Bible may be right and our lives have a corrupt nature that only God can restore? Consider...

> *"Wretched man that I am! Who will set me free from the body of this death?"* —Paul (Romans 7:24) (answer in verse 25)

How would you answer the belief that mankind is basically good and can solve his corrupt nature without God's salvation?

REASON TWO: We have a real live supernatural devil against us.

All human beings have an enemy, the devil, who lies to us, who tempts us in areas of our weakness, who tries to destroy our lives. The Bible warns us about the devil.

> "Be of sober spirit, be on the alert. Your adversary, the devil, prowls about like a roaring lion, seeking someone to devour."
> — Peter (1 Peter 5:8)

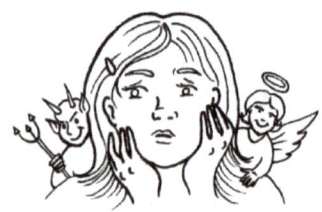

> "... He was a murderer from the beginning, and does not stand in the truth, because there is no truth in him. Whenever he speaks a lie, he speaks from his own nature; for he is a liar, and the father of lies." — Jesus (John 8:44)

> "... Satan disguises himself as an angel of light."
>
> (2 Corinthians 11:14)

> "People need to "come to their senses and escape from the snare of the devil, having been held captive by him to do his will."
>
> (2 Timothy 2:26)

Satan uses other people to pressure us. He uses our unmet needs for love, acceptance, significance, and belonging to pressure us to have those needs met in the wrong ways or places. He uses the excuse-making and negative thinking of our own minds to convince us to give in to what we see as ok but is hurtful in the end. (Proverbs 14:12)

When people learn that you believe in a devil, you may hear some people say:

"You are old fashioned and outdated to believe all that stuff about a devil. He is a myth out of the past. People in the modern scientific world don't believe in a devil."

A response to this is:

If there is a God, and if He has spoken truth into our world, and if He says there is a devil, then there must be one. Take a long hard look at the evils of the world. What is your explanation for them? Has God spoken truth into this world, or hasn't He?

I'd like to hear your explanation for how evil entered this world. How would you answer people who don't believe in the devil?

REASON THREE: We need to maintain contact with the all-powerful and loving God who can help us.

All human beings have the potential to know God. He wants to be involved in our lives to help ensure that we can cope with life in an evil world. God can help me in this life to be growing into the wonderful, mature person He designed me to be. We can overcome our fears and sufferings by learning to trust in the only power who can save us and bring us to complete wholeness. This wholeness will be completed, not totally in this age of the world, but in the next. We need to know God.

The Bible tells us that God is our needed resource for survival. What does God provide for us according to the following verses?

> "... His divine power has granted to us everything pertaining to life and godliness, through the true knowledge of Him who called us by His own glory and excellence. For by these <u>He</u> has granted to us His precious and magnificent promises, in order that by them you might become partakers of the divine nature, having escaped the corruption that is in the world by lust" ——Peter, a disciple of Jesus (2 Peter 1:3-4)

God revealed who HE IS to Moses:

"... behold, the bush was burning with fire, yet the bush was not consumed... God called to him from the midst of the bush, and said, 'Moses, Moses!'"

"And he said, 'Here I am.' Then He said, 'Do not come near here; remove your sandals from your feet, for the place on which you are standing is holy ground.' Then Moses hid his face, for he was afraid to look at God. Then Moses said to God, 'Behold, I am going to the sons of Israel, and I shall say to them, The God of your fathers has sent me to you.' Now they may say to me, 'What is His name?' What shall I say to them? And God said to Moses, 'I AM WHO I AM'; and He said, 'Thus you shall say to the sons of Israel, I AM has sent me to you.'" (Exodus 3:2-6, 13-14)

Jesus claimed the same name, "I AM", for Himself (John 8:58). It is said of Jesus that He is "God with us". God has come to help us be overcomers. He Is the one we need—the way, the truth, the life (John 14:6).

Some may say:

"There is no God." Or,

"God cannot be known." Or,

"Grow up; we don't need God."

Here is an answer to the question:
Does God exist and can we know Him?

No one can say God does not exist because no one knows everything. It is possible that He exists outside of what we know. One can say that we can't know God, but to do so, one must deny that Jesus lived, died and rose bodily from the grave. His resurrection is convincing evidence that He was from God. If Jesus was from God and said that we can know God, why then should we not believe what Jesus said? Some people do not believe in God because they say that if He existed and was good and all-powerful, He would do something to destroy evil. Since evil exists, then God must not. But it is possible that God exists and has good reason for allowing evil.

Besides, God does have a plan to destroy evil and make a world that is completely good.

> *"But according to His promise we are looking for new heavens and a new earth, in which righteousness dwells."*
>
> *(2 Peter 3:13)*

How would you answer someone who says, "Why do you believe in God?"

These then are three reasons for a survivor guide:

1. We have corrupted, self-centered natures.

2. We have a real live supernatural devil against us.

3. We need to maintain contact with the all-powerful and loving God who can help us.

This survivor guide cannot give you all you need to know because survival is a lifelong learning process; but things you need in order to survive can be mapped out for you, and if you stick by them, they will help you get to where you want and need to go. Many people have dreams of how they want life to be, only to have these dreams vanish by life's stark realities.

Seek your journey and contentment and joy in Christ. Through your relationship with Him, win the battle over self, the devil and ignorance.

HOW TO SURVIVE

There will be **four ways** to survive discussed in the following pages.

WAY ONE: If you are not a committed Christ follower, become one.

> "Jesus spoke to them, saying, 'I am the light of the world; he who follows Me shall not walk in the darkness, but shall have the light of life.'" (John 8:12)

> "My sheep hear My voice, and I know them, and they follow Me."
>
> — Jesus (John 10:27)

Being a follower of Christ Jesus is where the ability to be a survivor begins.

"Christ gives me the strength to face anything." — Paul, God's appointed messenger, who suffered many hardships. (Philippians 4:13)

Here is what the Bible says about the importance of having Jesus in your life.

> "He who has the Son has the life; he who does not have the Son of God does not have the life." — John, a beloved disciple (1 John 5:12)

Make sure you belong to Christ Jesus.

How?

Have you ever asked Him to forgive you, to give you His promised gift of righteousness and life, and His Spirit?

Do you have faith to believe that He has done it?

Are you, or are you not, committed to Christ and His leadership in your life? This means, do you have a desire in your heart to do what He says?

If someone asks you to explain to them how they could be saved and be sure of going to heaven, what would you tell them? How do you know you told them the right thing?

The way to become a Christ follower is to pray and ask God to save you, have faith that he has done it, then seek to obey His word out of the love he has given you by His Spirit. And keep growing in your understanding of what all this means.

__WAY TWO: Make an effort to read at least one chapter of the Bible every day. And think about what you read.__

Decide on a time and just do it!

Here are chapters I recommend for you to read:

- ❖ Gospel of John (all chapters)
- ❖ Proverbs (chapters 1-7)
- ❖ Romans (all chapters)
- ❖ Psalms (chapters 1-23)
- ❖ James (all chapters)
- ❖ Zephaniah (all chapters)

Read and re-read the recommended chapters until you understand them. Ask God to help deepen your understanding.

Why regularly read the Bible?

What happens if you go without daily physical food?

Spiritual food keeps our inner spirit and relationship with God alive. What happens without it?

Don't neglect God's trusted food for your soul!

> *Jesus said,* "It is written, 'Man shall not live on bread alone, but on every word that proceeds out of the mouth of God.'"
>
> *(Matthew 4:4)*

THE BIBLE

The next five statements are things people have said about the Bible:

- ❖ "The Bible is an outdated book, not relevant for our modern age."

- ❖ "The Bible is only human ideas, myths to help the people of ancient times explain life."

- ❖ "The Bible is made up of stories the Christians invented to get people to believe their story about Jesus."

- ❖ "The Bible is full of discrepancies and cannot be trusted as truth."

- ❖ "The original written text has not been passed on accurately to us."

These, along with other opinions, are given to persuade us that the Bible ought not be trusted as God's inspired Word, and that we are ignorant or foolish to believe it.

How would you answer the five arguments on the previous page?

One answer is this:

There will never be 100% proof that it is God's word, which was given to tell us how we can be saved from an evil world and have eternal life in God's Kingdom. But there is enough **evidence** to make it reasonable for one to believe that the Bible—a collection of books—is from God. I don't know about you, but such evidence is sufficient for me to put my faith in what the Bible says.

Some may ask, "What evidence?"

Here are things you should know:

1. Many historical particulars of the Bible have been confirmed by archaeological finds.

Do you know some examples?

Where could you go to find out?

2. Fulfilled prophecies and promises are unexplained except by Divine foreknowledge and power to bring them about.

Do you know what these prophecies are?

3. Jesus said that the Scriptures are from God. His testimony to this fact is verified as true by the sign of His resurrection from the dead; a fact that has never been convincingly refuted.

How do you know the resurrection happened? Check out Lee Strobel's book, *The Case for Christ*.

You are in solid company to put your trust in the Bible and to make it your guide for salvation and right living.

> "All Scripture is inspired by God and profitable for teaching, for reproof, for correction, for training in righteousness."
>
> (2Timothy 3:16)

WAY THREE: Find a Christ-honoring fellowship group and become a part of it.

❖ Be as regular as you can in attendance.

❖ Develop a treasured friendship with one or more in the group.

❖ Spend time together.

Why should I be in a fellowship group?

By association with people of like mind, our lives are more easily kept on track with our Christian goals, values and life-styles. We help each other grow.

Here are some things God says about the importance of fellowship:

> "Do not be deceived: "Bad company corrupts good morals." (1Corinthians 15:33)

> "Iron sharpens iron, So one man sharpens another." (Proverbs 27:17)

> "and let us consider how to stimulate one another to love and good deeds, not forsaking our own assembling together, as is the habit of some, but encouraging one another; and all the more, as you see the day drawing near." (Hebrews 10:24-25)

What does God teach you in the above verses?

Here are ideas of some groups you could join:

A church small group; a young college or career group in a church; a Christian group on campus, such as Cru or Navigators; a discussion group that meets in a home or at a cafe, etc.; personal friends you hang with who are strong believers in Christ and who "walk the talk".

Some may laugh and poke fun at you for attending a religious group.

This puts pressure on you to steer away from the fellowship you need, for fear you will not be accepted by others.

They may want you to join with them in their activities, some of which may not be pleasing to God, or be what you want.

To those who poke fun, you may say:

"I respect your choice not to belong to a group like this, but I choose to belong because..."

It is good to have some friends outside The Faith; to accept their invitations to do things with them; and to care about them. Do your best to accept people. But do not enter into activities with them that would lead you to violate your moral God-given convictions. Be strong to excuse yourself and leave. It's ok to say "you go ahead, but this is not something I would like to do."

Be a leader, not always a follower.

When tempted by others to not attend your fellowship group, remember the choice of Moses:

> "By faith Moses, when he had grown up, refused to be called the son of Pharaoh's daughter; choosing rather to endure ill-treatment with the people of God, than to enjoy the passing pleasures of sin; considering the reproach of Christ greater riches than the treasures of Egypt; for he was looking to the reward." (Hebrews 11:24-26)

THE CHURCH

What is the Church?

It is the world-wide body of people that Jesus created. He has put all believers into the church by causing them to possess His Spirit. If you are a believer, you are a part of the church. Try local churches out and find one that you like. The church's purpose is to fulfill the mission of Jesus and to help one another grow in the faith. The church is a way to stay connected to Christ and be a part of His work in the world. Many churches are changing to fit the times in which we live, but the message must remain true to the Bible. No church is perfect. But Jesus loves the church.

You can substitute the word "church" for "body"

> "For by one Spirit we were all baptized into one body, whether Jews or Greeks, whether slaves or free, and we were all made to drink of one Spirit. For the body is not one member, but many." (1Corinthians 12:13-14)

Why do churches differ?

There will always be differences between you and other people. God has allowed great variety in worship and ways of doing things. He puts in the hearts of people to serve each other in different ways. This variety assures that there is something for everyone.

Some churches reach people whom others may not. Yet, the church is one church and is unified in her faith that Jesus is the Son of God and Savior of the world. When Christ returns, He will take His one multi-varied church to be with Him forever.

> "For God has not destined us for wrath, but for obtaining salvation through our Lord Jesus Christ, who died for us, that whether we are awake or asleep, we may live together with Him." (1Thessalonians 5:9-10)

WAY FOUR: Know what you believe and why.

You will run into many ideas and beliefs that differ from your own. Reason, common sense, and God's word are good standards by which to test these. The Bible is a good place to go if you are confused about what is or is not true.

You don't need to accept everything at face value.

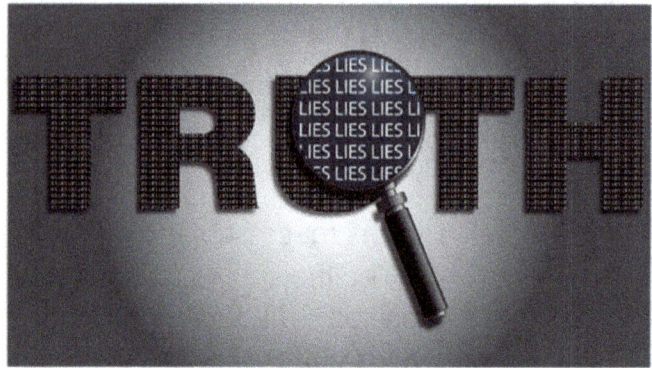

Learn to understand and evaluate everything, rejecting anything you find to be false, and accepting those things you find to be true.

For example, some truth may be found in other religions besides Christianity, though not everything is to be accepted. There is always something to learn from other areas that differ from your own.

Work to develop a Christian world view and learn to be gracious toward those who differ with you. Read Romans Chapter 14.

The Bible gives guidance in dealing with people and knowledge where there is a mixture of truth and error.

> *"See to it that no one takes you captive through philosophy and empty deception, according to the tradition of men, according to the elementary principles of the world, rather than according to Christ." (Colossians 2:8)*

> "Let your speech always be with grace, seasoned, as it were, with salt, so that you may know how you should respond to each person" (Colossians 4:6)

> "Put on the full armor of God, that you may be able to stand firm against the schemes of the devil." (Ephesians 6:11)

Truth is one thing we are to put on. Know the truth and why you believe it.

KNOW WHAT YOU BELIEVE AND WHY CONCERNING TRUTH AND TOLERANCE:

Some may say:

"There is no such thing as absolute truth. It is wrong to make truth claims of any kind."

You may respond:

"Is this statement you have just made an absolute truth? Have you just made a truth claim? If you have, then there are absolute truths because you have just given one."

WHAT IS ABSOLUTE TRUTH?

An absolute truth simply means that there are some things that are real and they are the same for everyone. For example, if God is real, then He exists absolutely and the fact that some may disagree, will not make His existence go away.

Also, if God makes a statement that agrees with reality, then what He says is true. For example, if God says that He created human beings, and if He really did, then His statement is absolutely true. If you say that you had pizza for lunch today and if you really did have pizza, then your statement is absolutely true.

Are there things that are true? For example, Was there really a person named Jesus? Did He really live, die on a cross, and raise again bodily from the dead? Is it true that if you get to know Him, as He says you can, that He will give you eternal life? If these events and sayings of Jesus are real, then they are true for all. It is not believing them that makes them true; they are true, whether you believe them or not. Although, believing them does, in a sense, cause them to become a reality for the believer.

Some may say that the thing wrong with absolute truth is this:

"If someone doesn't agree with it, then you are saying they are wrong. You must be tolerant of others and their beliefs and lifestyles. You have no right to say, 'I am right and you are wrong'. That is being intolerant, even immoral. You need to affirm that everyone is right in what they believe and in how they live their lives."

An answer to this:

Yes, I agree we should be tolerant. Tolerant is defined as respectfully listening to what others have to say, understanding them, and giving them the right to believe what they want, even if I disagree. I will not force the truth on them, but if they freely choose to accept the truths that I believe because they see valid reasons for them, as I do, then how am I being intolerant?

As for the fact that truth exists, which makes those who don't agree with it to be wrong, what is wrong with that?

We observe this in our world every day. For example, take a 12-inch ruler as a standard of measure.

If something truly measures 10 inches long, and another says, "no, to me it is 8 inches," am I to tolerate what they say as being just as right? To live in such a world would be confusing and chaotic?

A good definition of truth:

Truth is, whatever is real. Truth actually exists. Statements that agree with what exists and is real are true statements.

Some may say:

"Truth is what is real for me and it may not be real for you. Something may be true for you, but it may not be true for me. Truth is relative."

An answer to this:

Some have used the example of blind men, each one touching a different part of an elephant.

One person says an elephant is like a long, twisting muscular arm (describing the trunk). Another may say, no, an elephant is like a large tree trunk, sturdy and strong (a leg). Another may say, no, an elephant is like a rope (the tail). Another may say, no, an elephant is like a large rough wall (its side). Each one is right in saying what is true for them.

Truth can be relative. But they are wrong in knowing the absolute truth.

The truth, what is real, is the whole elephant. They only know part of the truth. Truth can be both relative and absolute.

What is true for me and what is true for you may not be true at all, or it may be. But that is beside the point.

The point is that there is such a thing as reality or truth, whether or not we agree with it, experience it, or believe it. What is true for me and what is true for you may be different, but there is a truth that is the same for both of us, if we only knew it. God is such a truth. So is His word, the Bible. So is the resurrection of Jesus. Our task should be to discover truth.

> "Thy word is truth." — Jesus (John 17:17)

How would you answer these questions:

- What is the truth?
- Is there absolute truth?

Jesus affirmed that there is absolute truth, and that others needed to know it.

"Jesus said... 'I am the way, and <u>the truth</u>, and the life; no one comes to the Father, but through Me.'" (John 14:6)

"Pilate therefore said to Him, 'So You are a king?' Jesus answered, 'You say correctly that I am a king. For this I have been born, and for this I have come into the world, to bear witness to <u>the truth</u>. Everyone who is of <u>the truth</u> hears My voice.'" (John 18:37)

He gets us!

KNOW WHAT YOU BELIEVE AND WHY CONCERNING MORALITY

Some may say:

"What is moral or right for me may be different from what is moral or right for you. You can't judge me and should not judge me."

Here is one way to answer such a belief about morality:

Yes, there is truth in the above statement.

However, what makes something moral, or not, is standards that are set by the society in which you live. You cannot be a law unto yourself and do whatever you want.

Furthermore, God sets the ultimate standards for what is moral, or not, based on His own perfect character. It is not I who judges you, or you who judges me, but God is the supreme judge of whether or not we are moral.

There is moral truth. Morality is in the world because God is a moral being and we are created in His image. We answer to Him. Here are Bible passages that speak of God and morality:

> "Now the Lord said to Moses, 'Come up to Me on the mountain and remain there, and I will give you the stone tablets with the law and the commandment which I have written for their instruction.'" (Exodus 24:12)

> "And this is His commandment, that we believe in the name of His Son Jesus Christ, and love one another, just as He commanded us." (1John 3:23)

> "But for the cowardly and unbelieving and abominable and murderers and immoral persons and sorcerers and idolaters and all liars, their part will be in the lake that burns with fire and brimstone, which is the second death." (Revelation 21:8)

God is not throwing a blanket on fun, but is defining areas that will either give us an enjoyable life, or destroy us. Fun is enjoying all things in God's created world that are not wrong in His eyes.

Things that are wrong can seem like fun, but in time we find out that they cause hurt and loss. (See Proverbs 16:25)

One area of morality that interests most everyone is our sexuality. It might interest you to know that the Bible provides guidelines for proper and improper sexual encounters. For our protection, God reveals sex that is off limits.

Here is a list of immoral sexual behaviors: prostitution (sex for money or some other payment), rape, incest (sex with family members), homosexuality, lesbianism, bestiality (sex with animals), adultery (being unfaithful to your married partner), whoredom (any sex without being married).

(See Leviticus 18 for some of these.)

> "For this is the will of God, your sanctification; that is, that you abstain from sexual immorality" (1Thessalonians 4:3)

Sex is right and good when it is restricted to the marriage relationship.

> "Let marriage be held in honor among all, and let the marriage bed be undefiled; for fornicators and adulterers God will judge." (Hebrews 13:4)

How can you say NO to persons who want you to have sex?

You want to be able to say "no" and mean it, and at the same time not be offensive to the person you say "no" to.

Here is one way:

"I have made a commitment to God and myself that I will keep God's standards for me as best I can. I chose to make this commitment and I want to keep it. It has nothing to do with you, but with my choice."

"I need you to respect my decision and to help me keep it. It is not always easy, and that is why I need you to help me."

NOTE: If someone keeps pressuring you, do they really care about you or only about themselves? Maybe you need to rethink building a serious relationship with them.

In the Bible, a man named Joseph faced this pressure. You can read about it in Genesis Chapter 39. Here is what he said:

> " How then could I do this great evil, and sin against God?" — Joseph (Genesis 39:9)

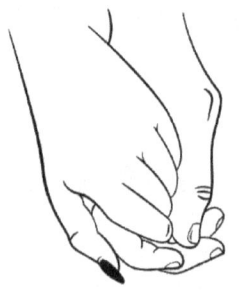

Can you think of a good way to say no without making your friend feel rejected? Do you want to say no as a way of honoring Christ who loves you?

KNOW WHAT YOU BELIEVE AND WHY CONCERNING DATING AND MARRIAGE

God put man and woman together to complement one another, to meet each other's needs for companionship, and to reproduce themselves and have a family. God ordained marriage for our good and well-being, and to provide a healthy environment in which to raise children.

Finding a good mate in life is a concern that needs good judgment. God cares about your mate selection. Dating is part of the process. It is the time you spend with other persons getting to know them.

Selecting a mate for life is not an easy thing. When dating, you are considering that this person might be the one. Check things out by getting to know the other as well as you can before marrying. Don't let sexual or physical Intimacy, determine whether or not this person is right for you. We can easily get carried away with feelings we think are love, which are not, and then marry based on a mistaken idea of love. Don't let sexual and emotional involvement with someone ruin the potential for a good relationship later on with the person of your dreams. Ask God to guide you and help you find a good mate for life.

Here are things to consider in choosing someone you care to be with for the rest of your life.

Find out whether your families have similar backgrounds. Do you both have similar values? Are vocational and family goals agreed upon? Do each of you have the ability to adjust and adapt to differences? Do underlying anger problems or resentments exist? Do you have a good relationship with both sets of parents? Are bad habits revealed so there are fewer surprises later? Are health issues considered? Will this person make a good father or mother?

There is a short brochure, published by Rose Publishing, of 100 things to talk about in order to get to know the one you are seriously dating. It also includes a relationship risk quiz. Reference page 50 of this book for more information.

Remember, you will have feelings of love that draw you to another person, but God's kind of love is something we learn from Him and are able to practice in all relationships, including our marriage. It is different from that which we feel when we feel attracted to someone.

If people marry for love, and if love is unending, as the Bible says, then why do so many couples divorce? Did they have this unending love? They felt like they did, but must not have, or it would have continued. Knowing God's love helps ensure a successful relationship.

What about living together before marriage?

It is understandable why so many do it, though many do not feel right about it. Lots of young people today grow up in homes that are divided and where healthy role models were not seen. No wonder they do not trust marriage and think they better try it out first before they jump into it. But modern social studies seem to reflect that living together is not necessary in order to make sure you have the right mate. Pray and seek God's will and blessing. He will guide you. Also, become the kind of person God says you can be, as taught in God's word, and you will be a better fit for any relationship. And, marry someone who is spiritually your equal or better. Don't think you can win someone to your faith later on. This may be hard, especially if you allow yourself to get entangled with a person who does not believe as you do. Find out early and stick to your convictions.

> "Do not be bound together with unbelievers; for what partnership have righteousness and lawlessness, or what fellowship has light with darkness?" (2 Corinthians 6:14)

KNOW WHAT YOU BELIEVE AND WHY CONCERNING VOCATIONS

Choosing a vocation is hard for many. God designed us to work, and He knows what we are fitted for. Ask God to guide you and tell him you want His will for your life. Determine your likes and interests, for God has put certain desires in you. There are tests you can take to help you discover what you may be suited for and family and friends who know you well may be able to give you advice; but most of all look deep into your heart. Follow these natural heart desires and see where they lead. Doors may open or close ahead of you. Walk through the open doors and consider a closed door as God wanting you to go in a different direction, unless you know this is what God wants for you, in which case you must have perseverance to overcome obstacles. All occupations that are not evil are acceptable to God and they all are a way of serving others with the gifts and talents God gives you.

> "Whatever you do, do your work heartily, as for the Lord rather than for men" (Colossians 3:23)

Remember, wherever you are and in whatever you do, you are one of God's gifts to help meet needs in a world of hurting people. Your job is a service to others' needs.

God blesses some people with riches, but making money is not as important as being happy or content in what you do. And whatever you do, honor God with good hard and honest work, endeavoring to please your boss and God. Be concerned for the success of others, as much as for your own.

And let no one say that being a stay-at-home parent is a waste of your life. Raising children to be great people, able to cope with life's problems, and able to contribute something good to the world and to God's kingdom, is a noble and challenging task. It is worthy of the best effort you can put forth.

How does a person know God's will?

(Who does He want me to marry? What job does He want me to have?)

God's will for how we are to live our lives each day is found in the Bible. In other areas, God leaves it up to our choice and expects us to make wise decisions. Choose a course and follow it and trust God to direct as you proceed.

I like the illustration of a ship in the water. As long as the ship is moving, it can be steered in the direction you want it to go. So, it is with God and His will. Choose something you like, even if you are not sure it is the right thing for you. Trust God to guide you.

KNOW WHAT YOU BELIEVE AND WHY CONCERNING HUMAN NATURE. WHO ARE WE?

Genesis Chapter 3 tells us what human nature has become as a result of the choice to put ourselves ahead of God.

Genesis 3:5 says we have become like God knowing good and evil.

Genesis 3:8 says we know things are not right with us so <u>we want to cover up and hide from God and each other.</u>

Genesis 3:9 says that we hide from God because <u>we fear His punishment for our wrongdoing.</u>

Genesis 3:12-13 says <u>we blame others</u> instead of taking responsibility for our own choices and actions.

Genesis 3:16-19 says the earth is cursed and <u>we die because of our sin.</u>

This is a good description of our godly nature gone bad.

Because we wrestle with a nature gone bad, we all falter, make mistakes, and do wrong things. However, for those who know Christ Jesus, we are forgiven when we fail. We must accept this forgiveness and go on. Satan would like to speak things into our mind, such as, "it's too late. You've blown it.

You might as well give in and keep doing what is wrong." No! Don't believe the lie. Start over again from this point and keep trying to do what is right in God's eyes.

God created us good, but due to the misuse of our freedom of choice, our relationship with God has been marred and needs to be restored. We have experienced evil and we cannot overcome it on our own. We need God. He has provided the answer in Jesus Christ, the perfect human, who has come to restore our lives back to the good image of God.

> *"Then who can be saved?" ... Jesus said, "The things impossible with men are possible with God." (Luke 18:26-27)*

We all err. When you goof up, confess your fault, then thank God for His forgiveness, which He can grant you because of the death of Christ who paid your debt; then be guilt free as you continue on your day-to-day journey.

If you still feel guilty, have you really believed that God has forgiven you? If others are involved, you need to make things right with them.

> *"If we confess our sins, He is faithful and righteous to forgive us our sins and to cleanse us from all unrighteousness." (1 John 1:9)*

> *"There is therefore now no condemnation for those who are in Christ Jesus." (Romans 8:1)*

> "... we have an Advocate with the Father, Jesus Christ the righteous" (I John 2:1)

Here is one more thought about our humanity.

I know you will at some time be asked to entertain the idea that <u>Darwin's theory of evolution</u> is true. It is helpful to know that many scientific presentations today by top scientists are now refuting this theory. In fact, a world renown atheist has recently stated that he changed his mind and now believes in a Creator because of new evidence science has been presenting. The physical world and Bible are both from God. Good science and good Bible interpretation should agree.

KNOW WHAT YOU BELIEVE AND WHY CONCERNING FRIENDS AND CHURCH

I know that I have already said some things about the church, but we live in such a mobile society that people often lack roots and solid life support. The church is a very important source if we are to be survivors. So, let me revisit the subject with you one more time and give helpful advice, including some thoughts about developing friends.

When people move to a community, they somehow expect to find a church like the one they left.

Or, if they begin attending a church they feel like an outsider. The facts are: you will rarely find a church like the one you left; and, new friendships are not automatic. Even so, the church is one of the best places to go to meet new people and build meaningful relationships. However, it will take understanding and effort on your part. Feelings of being a stranger and not receiving a warm welcome are true for many who begin attending a church. It takes courage to begin attending any new place.

HERE ARE 10 THINGS TO THINK ABOUT CONCERNING CHURCH AND FRIENDS:

(1) Visit as many churches as you like, looking for a church that teaches and preaches the truths of the Bible; a church that talks about Jesus being the Lord of our lives and our Savior; a church where people seem friendly, smiling, sincere, and relaxed. You may not know this at first. If you have Christ's Spirit in you, He will give you a good sense about this. When you find a church that you think has potential for you, give it a month or two. Don't keep flitting from church to church each week.

(2) Ask questions. Ask people what they enjoy about the church. See if you are comfortable with the beliefs and people.

(3) Remember, no church believes everything exactly as you do, and no

church is perfect. Give and take applies in any earthly relationship. No person or church will agree with you on everything. The goal is to achieve oneness in Christ, even though there is not absolute agreement on every issue or point of doctrine.

4) Making friends is not easy. Many people already have a circle of friends, but some make time to include others. Accept invitations that are extended to you. See where they lead. If you keep rejecting invitations, don't expect people to keep reaching out to you.

Some tips on making friends:

Greet people, say hello, introduce yourself to them.

Ask anything that requires them to answer with more than a word, such as, "What kinds of things do you enjoy doing?"

Listen—show that you are interested in what they have to say. Listening to others attracts people to you because you make them feel important.

(5) You may need to find out who else is new in the church and invite them to do things with you. They may be seeking new relationships as much as you are. Friendships take time. Once you get involved in something and people see you are interested, new doors will open.

(6) Small groups are great places to socialize and make friends. Join one. It may be an exercise group, coffee group, Bible discussion group, or music group. Try it; If one group doesn't fit, keep trying. Don't let fears or disappointments control you.

7) Pick out someone you'd like to know or befriend. Invite them to lunch, or to golf, or to go on a run, or to do music... any hanging out that will begin building a potential friendship. If they do not respond, try another.

(8) If you seem to have a hard time making friends or being accepted, take an honest look at your own personality or behaviors. Is there an area you need to work on which is offensive or repelling to others? Ask for help.

(9) God's people ought to be loving and reaching out to new people, but unfortunately, it doesn't always happen as we think it should. Be patient, give people a chance, let your feelings and interests be known. Don't be like them; you learn to be the outreach person.

(10) The church is God's kingdom on earth, to do His work. If you are a believer, then you belong to Christ and His body. Get in there and help make it the best it can be

for the glory of God. You can do a lot of good and you can reap a lot of good.

> "So then, while we have opportunity, let us do good to all men, and especially to those who are of the household of the faith." (Galatians 6:10)

FINAL EXAM

1. Can you tell three reasons why this survivor guide was created?

2. Can you name the four ways to be a survivor?

PARTING COMMENTS

YOU ARE A WINNER

The important things I have learned in life have come through evaluating my experiences—good and bad; from involvement with God—the church—the Bible; and through listening to other people - all people. God thinks you are wonderful, with great potential, and so do I. But never ever forget: your worth and importance and significance in this world has less to do with your performance and most to do with your being loved by God. You, as one loved by God, are valued very highly just for being you. If ever you feel that your life is falling apart, that your insides are caving in, have faith in God and salvation through his Son. Stay in Christ—it is the safest and most peaceful place to be. Make sure He is at the center of your being.

"Therefore... let us lay aside every encumbrance, and the sin which so easily entangles us, and let us run with endurance the race that is set before us, fixing our eyes on Jesus, the author, and perfecter of faith..." (Hebrews 12:1-)

HANG IN THERE

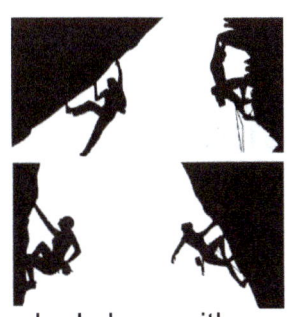

Yes, so much of life is good. God intended it to be so. And, you will have many questions, doubts, fears, failures, problems and temptations along the way. No one is the answer person for everything; but Jesus is. That is why I share with you four ways to be a survivor. They keep you in touch with Him. Those ways will help you to be victorious. Stick to those ways and they will provide you with the learning experiences, answers and support you need throughout your life. Talk to God as a friend and sort things out with Him, often. A get-away, quiet time with God is very helpful.

My greatest desire for you is that you make it to the next age of planet earth; the age of Christ the King.

100 Things to Know When Dating: Important Topics to Consider and Discuss by Rose Publishing

Product Details:

Published: March 13, 2015
Binding: Pamphlet
Pages: 14
ISBN: 978-1-89094-740-8
URL Location: https://www.hendricksonrose.com/p/100-things-to-know-when-dating/9781890947408

About the Author

Originally from Ohio, Jay Ashbaucher earned his undergraduate degree in education and a master of divinity degree before serving forty-four years in Montana as a pastor and Bible teacher. He served twenty years as a fifth step counselor and lecturer in an alcohol and drug treatment center, where he listened to countless stories of people's broken lives and struggles to achieve wholeness. Through them, he learned much about people and himself, which has helped in counseling individuals from all walks of life. He has enjoyed conducting grief classes, small groups, and teaching "Philosophy of Christianity" at a one-year wilderness Bible college. Now retired and living in Michigan, Jay continues God's ministry in his life through biblical teaching and mentoring as an author.

Other Books by Jay R. Ashbaucher

Out of Darkness into the Light: Learning to See Life from God's Point of View (Third Edition)

Building a Life with God Series:

BUILDING A LIFE WITH GOD: A Study for Individuals and Groups

Building a Life with God: Workbook

Upload Your Faith Series:

The Power of Life-Giving Hope in Troublesome Times

Faith

Perfect Love: The Eternal Gift

 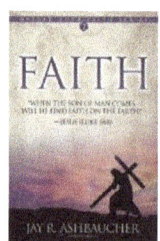 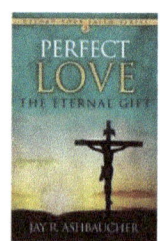